"What Did You Do at Nursery Today?"

A Guide to Your Child's Early Years

As I begin my journey on my first nursery day You may feel you miss me whilst I am away

But I'm going to busy having lots of fun Making friends, laughing lots and playing in the sun

So when you ask me what I did at nursery today I've been learning, growing and developing all through play!

Copyright 2019
Jo Callaghan, Liz Makins,
Charlotte de Lacey, Lucy Whitehead, Lucy Price

Acknowledgements

With thanks to the Fire Station restaurant, based just outside London Waterloo station, for allowing a group of us to sit for hours at a time, drinking copious amounts of tea and coffee while writing this book!

Thanks also to our families who have listened to us talk about our dream for some months and have supported us in achieving it; and to the wonderful friendships we have made along the way.

Last but not least, a big thank you to all the wonderful staff we have working in our settings, who have dedicated their lives to the world of childcare, and in giving your child the very best start in life!

The working party

Contents

Acknowledgements *4*

Foreword *8*

   Jo Callaghan and Liz Makins.. 9

   Charlotte de Lacey 10

   Lucy Whitehead 11

   Lucy Price 12

What is Your First Childhood Memory? *13*

What Should I Look for in a Nursery? *15*

Feeling Guilty? Don1t! *19*

Who is Looking After My child? *23*

How Are We Regulated? *25*

   Ofsted 28

The Importance of Early Years *29*

   Early Brain Development 29

How is My Child Learning Through Play? *32*

Speech and Language Development *35*

When Will My Child Write Their Own Name? *37*

When Will My Child Be Able to Count to Ten? *46*

   Maths 46

   Pre Maths 47

Meaningful Maths...49
When Will My Child be Able to Recognise Words? 51
Why All the Fuss About Outdoor Learning? 54

How will you keep my child healthy?................................... 59
  Physical activity..59
  Healthy Eating..62
  Mental health 65

Understanding the World... 66

What1s the Point of Messy Play? 70
  Play Dough..75
  Sand..76
  Water..77

A Word on Behaviour 79

What Happens Next? 81

Questions? 85

Foreword

Welcome to our wonderful world of childcare.

We are a group of childcare providers, and friends, who have worked collaboratively to devise a book for parents to help you understand 'what's the point of nursery?'.

We're all hugely passionate Early Years Educators who between us own 14 Ofsted-registered settings, with jointly more than 100 years of childcare experience.

Despite owning a variety of nursery schools, from Montessori to Forest School, we have successfully combined our breadth of knowledge to share with you everything we have learnt about providing your child with the very best possible start in life, so that you can get the most out of their formative years. We aim to give you, as parents, a guide on what to expect at nursery - the good, the brilliant and the messy!

Jo Callaghan and Liz Makins

We are sisters, born and bred in Essex where we have opened our nurseries. Jo had many years' experience, having opened eight nurseries previously and Lizzie was a primary school teacher for 23 years, most of which was spent teaching in reception age group.

It was our dream to work together and when we opened our first setting, we wanted to create an environment that we would have loved our seven children to attend. We feel we have achieved this in Munchkins. Our nurseries follow our own bespoke curriculum with a particular passion for outdoor learning and putting children at the centre of everything we do.

Jo Callaghan   Liz Makins

Charlotte de Lacey

My mum opened our first nursery back in 1982 in our house in Isleworth, but it quickly moved into our beautiful hall, where we have been ever since.

I took my Montessori Diploma, followed by my Early Years Professional Status and then took over ownership of the school in 2009 and have since opened 4 more settings in west London.

I am one of those lucky people who genuinely love their job, and it gives me great pleasure to share some of what I have picked up along the way with you here, to make your journey through your child's early years easier.

Lucy Whitehead

My 1st Nursery School is based in Southsea, Portsmouth on the South Coast. First owned by my parents and set up by them in 1983, I literally grew up with the nursery school all around me.

The nursery started in one room of our family home and eventually grew until it inhabited the whole of our detached Victorian home.

I went on to college and subsequently university and pursued a career in HR in London, until I had my first child in 2010. As my life and priorities had changed, I decided to re-train as a qualified Nursery Practitioner and became more involved in the family business once again, eventually taking over from my parents in 2013.

I now own 3 traditional all-year-round nursery schools, catering for children from birth to 8 years, and we pride ourselves on the true home from home environment we provide.

Lucy Price

Working with children has always been my dream career and after gaining qualified practitioner status I worked as a Nanny for five years. In 1997 I began working at Woodentots Nursery and was subsequently promoted to Deputy Manager and then Nursery Manager during the next three years.

In 2002, the opportunity arose to take on the overall running of the nursery and my tender bid was successful.

As Woodentots predominantly provides day care for military families we place a strong focus on supporting the many transitions children experience during their time with us, by providing a home from home environment where children are supported to develop their confidence, independence and resilience.

What's your First Childhood Memory?

In answering this, the majority of us will have probably picked a memory where the setting is in the comfort of our home with siblings, loving adults; or outside enjoying the natural environment.

These memories will usually consist of being with other children and most importantly we are playing independently, enjoying freedom and having fun.

Play is seriously fun!

Play incorporates every area of the curriculum that nurseries follow and cannot be separated from learning. A nursery environment has a wealth of opportunities for every child. A nursery will encourage your child to mix with their peers, explore new environments that stretch their imagination and enjoy a rainbow of stimulus which will encourage creativity, confidence, independence and develop enquiring minds.

We want to be a part of making happy childhood memories for your child within our nurseries, igniting the fires of knowledge and curiosity about the world around them.

Igniting the fire of curiosity.

What Should I Look for in a Nursery?

A fundamental part of your child's learning starts with the environment within which they find themselves. There is a huge variety of childcare providers across the country, which is great as this gives you so much choice to decide which environment is right for you and your child, because it is not a case of 'one style fits all'.

It is very important to research, shortlist and view as many nurseries, pre-schools, childminders as you think appropriate, to really get a feel of what they offer and how this might meet the needs of your child. This book will help guide you through this.

The world of childcare, as with some other industries, often works in a cycle and as with fashions, in terms of clothing and homes, often follows trends - "should we be using bright coloured plastic", "should we have a more natural calming environment" - honestly there is no right or wrong answer, it is largely down to parental choice.

There are a number of theorists within early years education, who influence how some settings approach the curriculum, for example Reggio Emilio and Montessori settings. We will touch on this in more detail later in the book, but essentially you need to get a 'good feel' for the setting you choose, and you will know when it 'feels' right.

What we do know, for example, is that babies can't see colour and will only see in black and white until they are around five months old.

Therefore, nursery settings catering for babies will often have a lot black and white sensory equipment and resources.

Beyond that, each childcare provider will follow their own beliefs, but fundamentally we understand that the most important thing you will want is a safe and calm environment to support your child's learning and development.

Our unique yurt in Wivenhoe

Sparking imagination

Engaging environment

Using real resources to stimulate young minds

Feeling Guilty? Don't!

From the minute you find out you are expecting a baby; most parents will start to feel guilt. Guilt about eating the wrong foods during pregnancy, exercising too much, not exercising enough, sleeping on the wrong side of your pregnancy bump, taking a bath that's too hot... the list is literally endless, and this doesn't end when the baby is born, in fact arguably it worsens. I didn't breastfeed, I co-slept, I didn't bond immediately etc, etc.

The question of work is a very personal thing. Some people aren't lucky enough to have the luxury of choice, they need to work for financial reasons and this affects around 77% of working mothers.

Some will choose to either work or stay at home and even though this a decision reached it will not be without question or guilt - "Have I done the right thing?", "Will my child feel abandoned?", "Am I doing enough for them?". You feel guilty when you are at work and guilty when you're not.

Even from a young age, children benefit from nursery

A common question from non-working parents is "Can I justify childcare if I don't really <u>need</u> it?". "What are the benefits?".

Again, this is a very personal choice and only one you, as a parent, can make - deciding what is best for your child.

However, it is well known that nursery schools can provide many benefits for children in their formative years. Studies suggest that significantly more pre- schoolers end up taking an academic route into university, than those without the same educational start.

Nurseries provide unique experiences

One of the biggest factors affecting and potentially easing a parent's guilt is, 'Who will look after my child when I'm not there?'.

This is often hardest for the parents, who are leaving their most prized possession for the first time in the hands of relative strangers. It is important for you, as the parent, to remember that no matter how hard you are finding it; having feelings of anxiety or stress can rub off on your child, making that transition harder.

It is also important to trust the people employed to care for your child (see 'Who is looking after my child'). You have done your research, you have sought recommendations, you have vetted and visited the nursery and the decision has been made.

It is now time to trust the trained experts and know that they are working in that profession because they truly care about the health and welfare of your child and have a desire to nurture them and watch them grow and develop, and they are passionate about bringing out the very best in each child.

This is the single most important decision you, as a parent, will take and as nursery providers we understand this. You naturally want to know your child is safe, well looked after, nurtured and above all else, happy.

Who is Looking After My child?

What is the difference between the various types of staff in an Early Years Setting?

You will hear staff in an early years' setting called all kinds of thing, some of which refer to their qualification level, some of which are just the wording that a particular type of childcare prefers; here is a brief summary;

- Teacher
- Early Years Teacher/Professional (EYT/P)
- Montessori Teacher
- Practitioner
- Early Years Educator
- Nursery Nurse
- Facilitator
- Play Worker

There are specific rules about the number of qualified and unqualified staff childcare settings are required to have, so you can be sure that the educational level of those teaching your child is of a high standard.

However, it is worth noting that unqualified does not necessarily mean 'worse' - a practitioner might just be starting out in their Early Years career, or may have years and years of experience but have no interest in being a student themselves, or may not have the money to pay for an expensive professional qualification; excellent staff come in all shapes and sizes, so do ask about the types of practitioner that your childcare setting employs.

All childcare workers are subject to government checks into their criminal record status, so that you can be sure that your nursery employs only those who are safe to work with your child.

Working with children is a vocation not a job

How Are We Regulated?

There seems to be a massive choice of early years provision out there, and it can be confusing understanding the difference between them all, and knowing which option is right for you. There are three main types of Early Years Provision, referred to as:

- *Day Nursery* (open all day, all year)
- *Pre-School* (open during school hours, with the same holidays as schools)
- *Childminder* (operating from within their home environment)

It is possible to mix and match your childcare - this does come with a health warning though, as children need routine and consistency to thrive, so having too many different influences can disrupt that.

The Early Years Foundation Stage Curriculum (EYFS)

All types of childcare providers, registered and inspected by Ofsted, are required to follow the Early Years Foundation Stage Curriculum (EYFS). The curriculum follows children through from birth to the end of Reception.

Class, at five years of age, and lays out the areas of learning at various ages and stages of development.

The curriculum is there to guide practitioners in understanding where children should be at any particular stage of their development and by providing stimulating environments and activities to help them grow and develop as individuals.

This may look like chopping and playing with fruit and vegetables. But it is so more...fine motor skills in preparation for writing, self-risk assessing, communicating with our friends, learning to share, mark making, maths for shape and size. The list is endless.

The EYFS is nonetheless open to interpretation, which is why each childcare provision is as unique as the children and families they serve, but there are a few legal requirements that all must offer;

- That the development of each child is regularly monitored to ensure that they are making appropriate progress through well-planned learning and development opportunities,
- That suitable staff are employed, to a set minimum adult/child ratio, and that each child has a named staff member as their 'key person',
- Access to the outdoors,
- And, of course, that children are kept safe and healthy.

Ofsted

All of the different types of childcare are also subject to quality inspections by OFSTED, The Office for Standards in Education.

You can find inspection reports online, and these can be used to give you an idea of the quality of the childcare you are looking at, but much more important is your gut feeling - "Does this nursery/pre-school meet your needs?", "Will your child be cared for and loved in the way that you want them to be?", "Will your child receive the early education that you feel they need and deserve?".

Ofsted inspections are a brief 'snapshot' in time of a nursery; and should be just one part of your research to find the right provision for you.

The Importance of Early Years

Getting it right during your child's earliest years will have a crucial impact on their future life chances. Emphasis tends to be placed on children's results throughout their time in compulsory education, with 61% of parents believing school is the most important learning period for children (National Literacy Trust, 2014). However, little is said about the stage from birth to five years, where the important foundations are laid for all further skills learnt.

Early Brain Development

During the period from birth to five years, rapid and intense growth of your child's brain will be seen and can only happen once in a lifetime. Here comes the scientific bit, so stick with us! The main components of our brain are called neurons and are usually what people are referring to when they say, 'brain cells'. Neurons transmit messages to and from the brain via electrical signals across structures known as synapses.

So how are brain cells developed? When your child receives positive interactions and when they are deeply involved in play experiences that interest them, the synapses form connections between one neuron's head to another neuron's tail. During the early years this process happens at double the rate of an adult brain, allowing children to learn things more quickly than is possible in adulthood.

Stimulating the brain with natural resources

As can be seen, this period of creating synapses is critical for learning new things and without practice and repetition, certain skills will disappear. For example, to create lasting skills in your child, such as learning to talk, it is imperative that their exposure to rich, meaningful language and words and the opportunities they have to practice are constant for it to be retained.

Such things as reciting nursery rhymes or reading stories will enable connections to be made and then strengthened on hearing the words again and again.

You're never too young to explore a book

Working with your child during the prime time of their brain development is a privilege. Whatever the approach used, we ensure we fully capture this brief but unique opportunity, to nurture, support and encourage the formation of your child's brain circuitry.

We achieve this through positive interactions and the use of age appropriate resources that are carefully planned to support your child's individual learning journey.

How is My Child Learning Through Play?

"Play is often talked about as if it were a relief from serious learning but for children play *is* serious learning" (Fred Rogers).

Through play, your child will make sense of the world around them and have the opportunity to discover, explore and experiment all through the medium of play.

It's learning through doing, creating those experiences through first-hand knowledge. There is never usually one outcome from this, as the activity evolves and adapts it can lead to many outcomes.

Resources are carefully chosen to stimulate young minds

A Crate .

What do you see?

Or do you see:

    A boat?
    A pirate ship?
    Going on a bug hunt?
    What is the weather like today?

Speech and Language Development

Children who have a strong vocabulary have a better start to their education and even enhance their life chances. This is fact.

Did you know that children who are read to every day until the age of five will have heard over 1 million more words than their non-reading peers?

Your child will need to hear a word a massive 500 times before they know, understand and start to use it.

As this is such a hugely important area, it forms a really big part of our work in early years, and skilled educators work very hard every day to fill children's 'word bank' with as much rich language as possible.

To support this important work, we would like to encourage you as parents to play an active part in developing these vital skills.

Children are the best role models

Here are our top tips:

- *Read to your child every day. If you do nothing else for your child but this, you will have done enough.*
- *Hold a running commentary on life in general - tell children what you are doing and what they are doing - for example; 'mummy is putting up a shelf, you are watching me from your high chair.'*
- *Name things for your child when they point things out or point things out to them yourself.*
- *Avoid using baby language - use 'dog' not 'doggie', 'thank you' not 'ta'.*
- *Repeat and mirror language, even babies babbling.*

- *Show you are interested in what your child has to say by using eye contact and getting down to their level.*

When Will My Child Write Their Own Name?

Pencil control is one of the most complex skills to introduce to children, therefore we have given careful consideration to how we support this.

In order for a child to hold and use a pencil correctly by the time they leave nursery to go on to school, there are many stages in which we provide a wealth of opportunities and experiences for the children to participate in, starting with our youngest children in the Baby Room.

Children need to develop control over their whole body and make as many large movements as possible, which will then enable them to gain control over the very small movements that are needed to write.

Here are some examples of how we support emergent writing at each age;

Children Aged 0 – 1 Years 'Tummy time'

It is essential to provide plenty of opportunities for babies to spend time on their tummy with books, treasure baskets, gloop and natural and interesting play items for them to explore. This, along with supporting the development of neck, shoulder and core strength, prepares the arms and hands for fine motor skills and supports early hand-eye coordination, both fundamental to the development of pre-writing skills.

Crawling

You should also encourage crawling for as long and as often as possible. This develops the arches in the palm of the hands, enabling the grasping of different sized and shaped objects. The arches direct the skilled movement of fingers and control the power of grasp.

Crawling also helps to promote your child's bilateral skills - the ability to use both sides of the body at the same time - supporting the essential skill of holding the paper steady with one hand and writing with the other.

Crawling promotes children's bilateral skills

Strengthening core muscles

Children Aged 1 – 2 Years
Large Motor Movements

Upper body strength and stability ensures effective arm movement and good postural control, which allows the hands to be used effectively when working on table top tasks such as writing and cutting with scissors.

The children have lots of opportunities to develop their upper body strength by rolling, catching and throwing balls, music and movement and obstacle courses.

Messy Play

Sensory play promotes the development of fine motor skills by encouraging the manipulation of materials, telling the brain where the hands are as they perform a task. The brain then coordinates these sensations to make small changes for precise coordination and muscle control.

Our nurseries use a vast range of media including paint, gloop, playdough, shaving foam and water to enable the children to begin making their own marks and discover different ways to manipulate the materials.

Sensory play promotes fine motor skills

Unusual ways of mark making

Children Aged 2 - 3 Years

Developing Hand Preference

By developing strength and dexterity in one hand, children will develop accuracy and speed when completing fine motor tasks, particularly handwriting. We provide many opportunities for children to practice activities that require a 'stable hand' and an 'active hand'. These include - pegging items on a line, washing the table, spreading butter on bread, pouring water from a jug, mixing items in a bowl and using bottles with pumps in the water tray.

Crossing the Midline

Being able to cross the midline - an imaginary line down the centre of the body - is the ability to reach across the middle of the body with the arms and legs.

Without this skill children may not be able complete a line of writing without either swapping the pencil to the other hand or turning their body to reach towards the opposite side.

We provide opportunities such as: tearing paper, popping bubbles, catching balloons, washing bikes in the garden, sweeping the floor and passing items round in a circle.

Creating large movements with water and chalk (crossing the mid line)

Children Aged 3 - 4 Years Finger Isolation

The ability to move each finger independently - is important to further develop a child's dexterity. It contributes to developing an efficient pencil grasp, as well as promoting the skills to type on a keyboard, tie shoelaces and successfully manipulate buttons and zips.

The children have lots of opportunities to access tweezers, chopsticks, pegs and tongs, to pick up and transfer items such as pom-poms and beads.

Practising finger isolation using pegs

Thumb Opposition

This refers to the ability to turn and rotate the thumb in order for it to touch each fingertip of the same hand. This is the main skill required to operate tools effectively and comfortably.

We encourage this by squeezing foam balls, hiding small objects inside tennis balls with a slit cut in them - requiring children to squeeze to open and shake the contents out, turkey basters and pipettes to squirt water in the water tray or to blow pom-poms across a table.

Thumb opposition

When Will My Child Be Able to Count to Ten?

Maths

The idea of maths can strike fear into many of us, but we want a new generation of children to grow up excited by, and interested in, numbers and maths.
In our early years settings, you will find maths woven through everything we do, and children learn about numbers and maths in a very practical, hands-on way.

You will already be familiar with many nursery rhymes and songs, all of which in many ways form our bread and butter at nursery; and are relevant and interesting for even the youngest of babies and toddlers. Here is an example in case you need some inspiration:

Five currant buns in a baker's shop Big and round with sugar on top Along came (insert child's name) with a penny one day, Bought a current bun and took it away.

Pre Maths

The idea of 'pre maths' might sound a little strange, but actually, there is a large and very rich wealth of learning that your child can and should access before the words 'maths and numbers' are ever mentioned. For example, did you know that puzzles, matching, sorting and ordering games are all giving your child key pre-maths skills of pattern recognition, sequencing, ordering, comparing, spatial awareness or problem solving?

This means that when they are ready to think about concrete numbers and all we can do with them, they are already experienced with many of the concepts we ask them to understand.

Not bad for a jigsaw eh?

Building a jigsaw involves shape, number, area and much more

Meaningful Maths

When maths is made meaningful for your child, their interest, motivation, and above all understanding, are very much increased.

For example, counting out how many plates we need for dinner has more meaning than counting dots on a page.

From the moment your child starts nursery, no matter how young they are, they will be taking part in carefully prepared and chosen activities and games to develop these life skills in a fun and interesting way that will bring maths alive.

Counting and sorting with everyday objects

The foundation of counting

You can even count in the wild

When Will My Child be Able to Recognise Words?

Many parents worry if their child might be unable to read basic words before going to school, but prior to this there is so much more that is needed to prepare a little one for the world of words.

In nursery we concentrate on Phase 1 of the letters and sounds curriculum. The other phases are approached once your child starts school. These include:

- *Environmental. The aim to raise children's awareness of the sounds around them such as listening walks, sounds lotto games, making shakers and comparing sounds. This promotes listening skills that are fast disappearing in our modern world*
- *Instrumental sounds - this aims to develop awareness of sounds made by various instruments and noise makers. Activities include comparing and matching sound makers and playing instruments to accompany a story*
- *Body percussion - Activities include singing songs and action rhymes, listening to music and developing a sounds vocabulary such as clapping out their name.*
- *Rhythm and rhyme - encourages children to begin the differentiation of words. Using stories such as the Gruffalo and Going On a Bear Hunt children are encouraged to finish words and sentences thus*

supporting children to recognise the similarities in words.

- *Voice sounds and oral blending - as children develop a listening ear, practitioners begin to break simple words down so that children recognise how a word is made up. For example, the adult holds up a cup and segments the word /c/u/p cup. The children can then enjoy clapping the syllables.*

The activities introduced to your child at nursery continue through to school, as lots of practice is needed before children become confident in their phonic knowledge and skills.

Listening to environmental sounds

Instruments develop an awareness of sound

Why All the Fuss About Outdoor Learning?

Here are some facts.

1. Children today spend only half as much time playing outside than their parents did.

2. Three quarters of UK children spend less time outdoors than prison inmates.

3. A government report in 2016 found that 1 in 9 children had not set foot in a park, forest, beach or any other natural environment for at least a year.

Shocking isn't it?

Balancing develops core muscles

In a world of technology and busy lives, children spend a huge amount of time in front of a device, and although this does have its positives, as we now live in an age of techno kids who know more about the internet than we do, a core essence of childhood is slowly depleting and "playing outside" almost seems to be a thing of the past.

Physical play is essential for a child's development

This is why outdoor learning is so important. It isn't just fresh air and pretty scenery. There are physical and mental benefits to spending time outside. Outdoor learning is a unique opportunity to develop and achieve confidence and self-esteem through hands-on learning experiences in a woodland or natural environment.

Hubble, bubble, toil and trouble

The outdoor "classroom" provides an ever-changing natural environment for each child to learn and thrive in.

Children are encouraged to explore and discover, risk assess and challenge themselves. Every child is taught respect for the environment, plants and wild animals who live there, as well as experiencing activities they could not do within the constraints of four walls, such as:

Tree climbing, shelter building, creating campfires, using tools safely, as well as creating positive relationships with themselves and other people - all under supervision, of course.

Outdoor learning gives the opportunity to develop new skills

Outdoor learning interweaves with the EYFS, as all areas of the curriculum are covered.

Outdoor physical activity also develops core muscles. By being physical and developing the core muscles, this in turn will help a child sit straight-backed for longer periods of time, hence retain attention, hence absorb information, hold a pencil correctly, hence learn to read and write.

Freedom to build confidence

Outside learning is not just about being physical. Our nurseries also give your child the opportunity to mark make, read, relax and chill, giving them time to think and use their creativity.

Stimulating senses

How will you keep my child healthy?

Physical activity

Children are more sedentary now than in previous generations, and we know that this can affect their mental health, ability to concentrate, as well as their fitness and their weight.

The Chief Medical Officer at The Department for Health says that children should be physically active for at least 180 minutes, or 3 hours, every day. This sounds like a lot, but there is so much great practice out there in early years settings that much of this target is done for you while children learn at the same time.

Here are a few examples that we hope illustrate the breadth of physical activity on offer to your child, apart from the traditional sports often on offer at nursery;

- **Parachute play**

Children use big movements to make the parachute move. They also co-operate with their peers, practice following a rhythm and follow instructions to co-ordinate the movement; they develop early literacy skills by singing songs and rhymes, develop perception skills and even take turns and share.

- **Tyre Play**

Tyres are an open-ended resource that are extremely versatile, but most uses involve heavy physical work - lifting, stacking, rolling, for example. Children in one of our nurseries have made a mobile ice cream shop, a fishing lake, an assault course and a car out of tyres recently.

- **Standing Instead of Sitting**

Simply removing chairs while children work, means that they engage their core muscles.

Independent physical play encourages self risk assessment

Healthy Eating

It is very important that children develop healthy eating habits from early in life, and again, nurseries and other childcare providers are very experienced at getting this right, even for the fussiest eaters!

Healthy body healthy mind

Good nurseries will also incorporate independence building programmes, such as serving their own food and pouring their own drink, and teaching about where food comes from and how it grows, into their healthy eating schemes - you would be surprised at how many children think that milk comes from the supermarket!

Even meal times are a learning experience

At nursery, children eat together, and often with staff, in a sociable way. This is so that mealtimes are valued and looked forward to as a time to share news and time with friends.

Some examples of healthy eating that you might see;

- *Only milk or water to drink at nursery, no juices or squash at all,*
- *Crudites, fruit and savoury biscuits as snacks,*
- *Homecooked balanced meals, high in protein and vegetables, low in salt and sugar, and meeting, and exceeding, government set standards.*
- *Special provision for children with allergies or dietary requirements.*

Mental health

Giving children emotional resilience, the ability to calm themselves when frustrated, and self-confidence, provide the foundation blocks for good life-long mental health and the Early Years are the most important life phase for your child to learn these skills.

Your child will be surrounded by adults who project predictable calm, who help them to identify and solve problems with peers and other adults, and who are responsive to their needs, value their input, and actively teach them about the emotions they might feel and how to recognize them in others.

Everyone needs time to chill

Understanding the World

'Understanding the World' sets the foundations for children's knowledge in science, technology, humanities and the natural world. A child's understanding of the world begins with them using all of their senses to explore familiar items to test what is and what is not possible.

Your child will receive an array of support in developing their understanding in a range of age-appropriate ways. Treasure baskets, often used with the youngest children, are filled with a wealth of different natural materials to promote exploration and discovery. This is an important stage in children becoming aware they can have an effect on their immediate environment

Through this type of play, babies discover how different objects taste, feel and sound, such as noticing that banging metal spoons together sounds different to banging a metal spoon with a wooden spoon or that a feather feels soft on their face and floats to the ground when blown, more slowly than a pebble.

Everyday objects stimulate the senses

As your child grows and develops, they further test their ideas using trial and error, observation and prediction. Observation is a key skill that allows children to learn more from what they are seeing. Whilst outdoors they may notice a worm does not have legs, the spiral lines on a snail's shell or the leaves changing colour on trees. This in turn prompts them to consider the similarities and differences between creatures or the seasonal changes that occur.

Awe and wonder!

We believe the role of a supportive, trained adult is crucial for your child to gain the confidence in thinking about what they are seeing or doing and to question the world around them.

Alongside this we ensure that plenty of new experiences are provided for your child to observe, question, predict and test their ideas, which helps them to think scientifically rather than simply accepting the world around them.

> As soon as children find something
> that interests them
> they lose their instability
> and learn to concentrate.
>
> Dr Maria Montessori

What's the Point of Messy Play?

Messy play comes in lots of different forms, playdough, water, sand, paint, shave foam, gloop, ice, playing with foods - for example rice, spaghetti etc.

Exploring spaghetti!!

It helps to instill imagination, creativity and exploration. Cognitive development in children occurs when their senses are stimulated, and messy play is so beneficial because it stimulates so many of their senses all at once.

Physical development - strengthening muscle control. Fine motor skills and hand eye co-ordination, resulting in eventually being able to hold a pencil and eat with a fork.

Communication - social interaction, shared discoveries even for those children too young to communicate through speech. By asking questions during the activity provides speaking and listening opportunities and encourages thinking skills.

Writing - Pincer movement, which is the grip we use to hold a pencil correctly, is developed through the manipulation of different materials, and the fingers finesse is increased by the different textures handled.

Social and emotional development - Supports the ability to play independently.

Messy play involves:

- *children using all their senses in the process of exploration, especially the sense of touch*
- *offering children plenty of opportunity to mould and manipulate materials*
- *not having a focus on making or producing something, therefore being more creative*
- *it practices good concentration skills*

Give a child the resources and they will create

This sort of play is important because it's very lack of a focus on making or producing something leaves your child free to explore all sorts of possibilities. It taps into children's innate curiosity about the world around them and their strong desire to explore and find out more.

By giving children messy play experiences, we give them the opportunity to explore materials fully. Messy play is also enjoyable and, most of all, good fun!

Messy play encourages children to play together

Explore, be curious and create

Play Dough

PLAY DOUGH

Concentration
Sustained periods of time creating, observing and altering model

New Vocabulary
Verbalising what they are doing / making, learn new words such as roll, squeeze, flatten etc.

Fine Motor Skills
Strengthens muscles in fingers by moulding, flattening, rolling, punching, squishing

Sensory
Play dough is relaxing, therapeutic and reduces stress. Adding liquid essence such as lavender heightens the sensory experience

Maths
Measuring ingredients, counting pieces, adding objects such as buttons to provide number concept, using shape cutters and moulds

Imagination
Through exploration it can be anything, a cupcake, snake or snowman, but once modelled it becomes transient and will develop along with the play.

Sand

Social Interaction
This area is often a 'gathering place', giving the child opportunities to develop social skills, turn taking and sharing

Maths
Mathematical language more/less, counting scoops of sand, different sized scoops and containers, weighing scales

Mark Making
Using sticks, fingers, or rakes to make their first marks in prepartion for writing

SAND

Imaginative Play
Creating sand castles, roads and bridges. Adding toy animals and cars creates imaginary worlds which can be changed with their interests

Physical Skills
Digging, pouring, kneading and moulding to build upper arm strength

Hand-Eye Coordination
Is promoted through using a spade to scoop sand into a bucket or truck

Water

Calming and Relaxing
Running hands through water often repetitive activity. Relieves tension

Maths / Science
Full, empty, half, less. Volume and capacity. How water changes substances, such as mud, flour, paint, coffee, tea, sand

Problem Solving
How to make objects float / sink. Why this happens. Just because an object is larger it does not mean it will sink.

WATER

Language Development
Drizzle, pour, drip, drench, damp, soaked, funnel, bubbly, trickle

Fine Motor Skills
Pouring, squirting, scrubbing, stirring and squeezing

Concentration
Often sustained periods of time concentrating especially when bubbles, food colouring or water creatures are added

Playdough

Sand

Water

A Word on Behaviour

There is so much to say about supporting children's behaviour in their early years that a whole book could be dedicated to it, as many have been, but that is not our purpose here.

There is, however, one fundamental principle that marks the difference between a calm child and a calm nursery, and a hectic, chaotic child or nursery - and that is engagement. When a child is engaged in their play and learning, and they are intellectually stimulated by skilful adults and exciting environments, they are disciplined.

Simply put, it is the job of the child carers to provide motivating and inspiring experiences for children to engage in and learn from, and when they do this successfully, you will see children working to their full potential, concentrating, co-operating, thinking and learning. You will not see signs of poor behavior, such as running around, shouting or hitting.

Friends for life!

What Happens Next?

What does school readiness mean to you, the parent? Being able to write your name? Reading a book?

Although you may feel this is wonderful and your child is shining, this is only a small part of what being ready for school is all about.

School readiness is about a balanced and even development - it's not heavily academic, focusing on the three prime areas - personal, social and emotional development; physical development; communication and language, which they will need before they can progress further.

Nurseries develop independence

For nurseries, school readiness means nurturing confidence, independence and developing an enquiring mind. This is achieved in so many different ways.

Nurseries encourage children from a very young age to explore new environments and activities so that they develop into confident learners. This can be achieved in a variety of different ways, including learning the words of their favourite nursery rhyme, finding their own shoes, putting on their coats, or successfully choosing their favourite book and retelling it in their own words.

We support those special milestones

What really makes a child ready for school?

- Being confident
- Gaining independence
- Developing a love of learning
- Enjoying books
- Interest in the world around them
- Social skills (sharing and turn taking)
- Empathy
  And so much more!

Every child is unique and learns at a different pace from their peers. In future life a Lawyer may not be able to wire a house and an Electrician may not be able to stand in court but this does not mean that one of them is any less than the other. The same applies in early years where every child's uniqueness and talent is applauded.

We want your child to be able, independent little explorers and learners - the key word here being independent.

Independent children are prepared for learning, they can better access the curriculum on offer and have a 'can do' attitude to life.

There are many ways that we support children to develop their self-care skills, that you can also mirror at home, all of which focus on daily practical life skills, such as;

- Helping with dressing tasks such as putting on their own coat, and pulling trousers up and down,
- Laying the table and serving and pouring,
- Tidying up,
- Opening and closing small pots/jars,
- Feeding themselves,
- Going to the toilet and hand washing.

It is not what you do for you children, but what you have taught them to do for themselves that will make them successful human beings.

The transition from nursery to school is an achievement in itself and should be celebrated.

Questions?

Want to know more or book a place?

You can get in touch with us in all of the ways listed below or better still come and visit us for a true feel. We are ready and waiting with advice, tips, guidance and, of course, information on how you can secure a place in one of our bespoke nurseries, forest school or holiday club.

Nursery Website
www.munchkins-nursery.co.uk

Munchkins Nurseries:
Wivenhoe
The Pavilion
King George V Playing Field
Wivenhoe
Essex CO5 6PE
01206 827126

wivenhoe@munchkins-nursery.co.uk
www.facebook.com/Munchkinsnurseryandforestschool

Laindon
30 Somerset Road Laindon
Essex SS15 6PE
01268 517311
laindon@munchkins-nursery.co.uk
www.facebook.com/MunchkinsNurseryLaindon

Dunton Fields
Sharp House Arterial Road Laindon
Essex
SS15 6DR 01268 543170
duntonfields@munchkins-nursery.co.uk
www.facebook.com/munchkinsnurseryduntonfields

Dunton Park
Warwick Crescent
Laindon
Essex
SS15 6JQ
01268 744004
duntonpark@munchkins-nursery.co.uk
www.facebook.com/munchkinsnurseryduntonpark

Brightlingsea
55 Victoria Place
Brightlingsea
CO 7 0AB
brightlingsea@munchkins-nursery.co.uk
www.facebook.com/munchkinsnurserybrightlingsea

Great Baddow
23-25 Church Street
Great Baddow
Chelmsford
CM2 7HX
01245 956616
baddow@munchkins-nursery.co.uk
www.facebook.com/munchkinsnurserybaddow

Munchkins Brentwood
Hogarth Primary School Brentwood
Essex CM15 8BG

Instagram

www.instagram.com/munchkinsnursery
www.instagram.com/wild_things_essex

www.ingramcontent.com/pod-product-compliance
Lightning Source LLC
Chambersburg PA
CBHW061740070526
44585CB00024B/2747